Friendship
411

NEVER
BORED

Written by Sue Gonzalez
Illustrated by Lisa Perrett

SCHOLASTIC INC.
NEW YORK TORONTO LONDON AUCKLAND SYDNEY
MEXICO CITY NEW DELHI HONG KONG BUENOS AIRES

FOR RAE GONZALEZ. YOU'RE NEVER BORING.

-S.G.

ISBN-13: 978-0-545-06569-6
ISBN-10: 0-545-06569-0

12 11 10 9 8 7 6 5 4 3 2   8 9 10 11 12 13/0

PRINTED IN THE U.S.A.
FIRST PRINTING, SEPTEMBER 2008

This is the end of boredom. It stops here! No more dull parties—not another do-nothing day ever again.
There are lots of mad cool things inside this book that you and your friends can do. It can be at a birthday bash, a slumber party, or on a rainy afternoon.
What are you waiting for?
Pick a page (any page) and get going.
You'll never be bored again.

The face looks familiar but you just can't remember the name!

To make this brain – boggling game, you'll need:

- ☞ Pieces of cardboard or poster board
- ☞ Tape or glue
- ☞ A bunch of magazines and/or newspapers
- ☞ Permission from an adult to cut up the magazines and newspapers

Here's how to make the game:

Look through pages of magazines and newspapers for photos of famous people to cut out. Cut them to about the size of the wallet photos you get with your school pictures. Use photos of celebrities from movies, TV, sports, politics, etc.

Tape or glue your celebrity photos on your pieces of cardboard. Number them. Make a master answer list with the name of every celeb written next to its number.

Here's how to play:

Each player gets a cardboard with the photos on it, a blank piece of paper, and something to write with. (Hint: If you have one piece of cardboard for each person playing, everyone can play at once.) Tell each guest to number his or her paper with a number for each photo.

The game starts and everyone has to write down the name ach celeb next to the number. The player who has identified ost photos correctly wins.

MY TEE FUN!

Love the logo design?
Hate the shirt?
Start cutting!
(Younger children should check with
your parents about using scissors.)

1. Lay your tee on a flat surface, front side up. Cut the sleeves off in a diagonal cutting both layers from the bottom of the sleeves to the neck.

4. Turn the shirt back to the front. Cut an even half oval that will fall along your collarbone.

2. Flip the shirt over. Cut a line from the bottom of the left arm hole to the bottom of the right arm hole. Make sure to only cut the back layer.

3. Cut from the center back neckline down to the back cut you just made. You should now have two flaps.

5. With scissors, narrow down the two back flaps so that they make ties you can tie around your neck.

6. Pop the shirt on and TIE the straps behind your neck. Done!

Easy Tie-Back Sleeves

This idea is especially good for tees with sleeves that are a different color from the rest of the shirt.

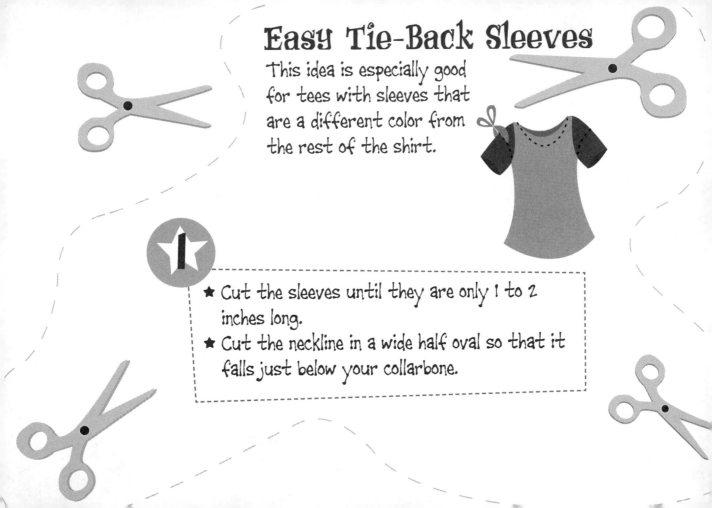

★ Cut the sleeves until they are only 1 to 2 inches long.

★ Cut the neckline in a wide half oval so that it falls just below your collarbone.

2

Cut two even pieces of string, ribbon, or cord. Start with about six inches for each piece.

3

Tie the string, ribbon, or cord tightly through the armhole and the neckline on both sides. This will pull the neckline straight across and give you a cute sleeve.

GET THE MESSAGE?

Once your parents say it's okay to instant message your BFFs, things start moving pretty fast. Will you be ready to handle all the IM shortcuts that your online pals will throw your way? You will once you check out this list.

AFK: Away from keyboard
Use it when you need to take a kitchen or bath break.

ASAP: As soon as possible
This one has been around a long time but it works here.

b/c: because. Because it's just faster to write it that way.

BFO: Blinding flash of obvious

BTW:	By the way
CYA:	See ya
G2G:	Got to go
IDK:	I don't know.
ILU:	I love you
JK:	Just kidding
L8R:	Talk to you later
LOL:	Laughing online or laughing out loud
LYLAS:	Love you like a sister
NM:	Not much
OMG:	Oh my gosh!
THX:	Thanks
w/:	with
w/e:	whatever
YGM:	You've got mail.

SO EMO!

While we're on the subject of IMs... Emoticons are little symbols you can make using your keyboard. Get familiar with them so you will know what they mean when one comes your way. Here are some of them.

:-) a basic smiley to show your happy face
     A quick little smiley can also be made like this :)
;-) a winking smiley
:-(a frowning face to show you're sad
     If you're really, really sad you can try this :-C
:'-(I'm crying.
:-@ What!!! Also :@
:-# I just got braces.
:-X I'll never tell.
:-D I'm laughing.

On the DL w/ Secret Codes

When your note is totally on the down low, meant for your BFFs' eyes only, you need a few good codes that only you and your best buds can crack. Try these.

Give 'em an Inch

For this code, all you and your friends will need is a ruler. Place a ruler on the paper. Write the letters in your message starting at the beginning of the ruler and then at every inch and inch-and-a-half mark. Circle the last letter of your message. Then fill in random letters all around. To decode, all your friend has to do is lay a ruler down, circle the first letter, and continue circling at every inch, and inch-and-a-half mark until she reaches the letter you have circled.

Easy As ABC, 123 Code

Write the ABCs in a line. Under each letter, write the numbers 1-26. (So a=1 and z=26). Then, instead of writing letters, you write the numbers. If you wanted to say: MEET ME AFTER SCHOOL, you would write: 13-5-5-20 13-5 1-6-20-5-18 19-3-8-15-12.

You'll Adore Semaphore

Semaphore was a flag code used between ships. Give a copy to your friends. Then they will know what you mean when you write:

M E E T   M E   A F T E R   S C H O O L

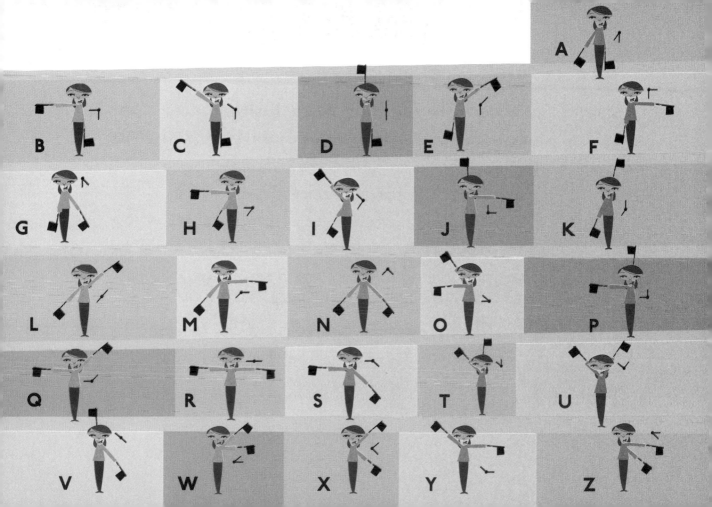

LOOKING GOOD!

The next time you get together
with a bunch of friends, maybe on a rainy Saturday
or at a sleepover, turn it into a Beauty Bonanza.
Try out the recipes here.
Chances are that you already have a lot of what you need in your fridge
or pantry (remember to ask before you grab it). Read this over
before you begin in case there are a few things you want
to get beforehand.
You'll need permission to do this activity because
each girl will have to wash her hair afterward.

AVOCADO SCRUB

To get started, you'll want
shining, soft, clean skin.
Try washing your face with this scrub.
You need: soft, ripe avocadoes, and cornmeal.
Cut open a ripe avocado (get the adult go-ahead
and adult help for this). Scoop out the insides.
Add 1 tablespoon of cornmeal for every
cup of avocado. Mix it all up.
Wet your face with water and then apply the scrub.
Wash your face with it and then
rinse well with water.

EASY (BUT MESSY)
FACE MASK

This is a facial mask that
you and your friends can apply after
your face scrub.

You need:

honey

egg

Mix together 1 teaspoon of honey for every 1 egg you use. The next step is going to get messy, so make sure you have lots of paper towels and/or regular towels around. Smear this goop onto your face and let it set for about a half hour. Then rinse it off with soap and water. Your skin will be smooth and soft. The mix will keep in the fridge for about two weeks.

BANANA AND HONEY
HAIR MASK

Hang on to that honey from your
facial. It's a natural moisturizer. It's been used on hair
and skin since the time of the ancient Romans and Egyptians.

For each girl you need:

ripe banana

2 tsps. plain yogurt

1/8 tsp. honey

2 tsps. sweetened condensed milk

Blend all ingredients until it looks like a thick smoothie.
Apply it to damp, towel-dried hair. Leave it on for at least a half hour.
Wash and condition hair as usual.

HOW TO GIVE THE BEST MANICURES

What Beauty Bonanza would be complete without a manicure? Here's how to do it.

NEVER-FAIL MANICURE

You need:

- nail polish remover
- medium grit nail file
- cuticle cream or hand cream
- soap and warm water
- orange or cuticle stick
- soft cloth
- nail polish

Use the nail polish remover if there is any old polish on nails.

File nails to the length and shape you like.

Soak nails in soapy warm water for about 5 minutes.

Dry hands off and use an orange stick or cuticle stick to push back cuticles (never cut them).

Apply two coats of polish, letting the polish dry between coats.

End with a clear top coat, if you have clear polish.

Clean up any mistakes with a dab of nail polish remover on a tissue or cotton swab.

If you're feeling fancy, pick up nail stickers and/or nail glitter!

SIGN HERE! Sooner or later it's bound to happen. Someone will ask you to write a clever little message and sign your name. It could be a group birthday card, a yearbook, or a graduation or moving-up ceremony program. What do you write? Don't panic. Here are some tried and true sayings, rhymes, and autograph starters for you to make your own.

YOURS 'TIL... (PICK YOUR FAVORITE)
THE OCEAN WAVES
THE ICE SCREAMS
THE RAIN BOWS
THE AUTUMN LEAVES
THE BANANA SPLITS

Can't think.
Brain numb.
Good ideas won't come.
Broken pencil. Bad pen.
No strength
To start again.

(Write this one upside down)

By writing in it upside down.
Remember the girl who spoiled your book
Remember the girl in the town
Remember the girl in the city

Some write for pleasure,
Some write for pain,
I write only
To sign my name.

HOT IDEA* Take some photos of yourself or use photos you already have. You can tape your photo next to your name. If you have access to a scanner or copy machine, you can make lots!

ILMISU (I'll miss you.)

CUL8R (See you later.)

UR2gd24get (You are too good to forget.)

ILCUQT (I'll see you, cutie.)

Read
up
and
down

see
will
you
and

that
I
like
you

me
like
you
if

HOT IDEA* Buy a pack of sticky stars or a card of star stickers. Add a tail with a pen or marker. Write:

Way to go, shooting star!

Shoot for the stars,
You're a superstar!

You can go on this scavenger hunt without ever leaving the house. You do it while watching a movie together during a slumber party or on a bad weather afternoon.

Here's what you do:

⊛ Break into two or three teams.

⊛ Make a list of items. Each person or team gets a list that is different but equal in length and difficulty.

⊛ When a player spots one of the items on her list on the TV she calls out and crosses that item from her list.

⊛ The first person or team to cross off all items wins.

SOME SAMPLE LISTS

List 1	List 2	List 3
BED	NECKLACE	EARRINGS
RING	TRAIN	SCHOOL LOCKER
BIKE	TAXI	MICROPHONE
SCHOOL	BALL	REFRIGERATOR
PHONE	MUG	TOY
LAMP	HARD HAT	EXTERIOR OF HOME
CAR	DOLL	POLICE OFFICER
HAT	BOAT	SKATEBOARD

SLEEPING BAG MYSTERY

This is fun at slumber parties or while camping.

One person leaves the room. Everyone else changes sleeping bags, cuddling down deep inside of them so they can't be seen.

Someone calls to the person who has left the room to return. That person comes back and must guess who is in which sleeping bag without asking any questions.

How is this possible?

The guessing person is allowed to tickle any person hiding in a sleeping bag. She can also ask, "What animal are you?" To this, the hiding person must respond by making an animal sound.

As each person is correctly guessed, she must come out of her bag. The last person to be guessed becomes IT, the guesser in the next round of play.

MISSING MUCH?

Another version of this game is to send the girl who is the guesser out of the room. Everyone then switches sleeping bags except for one girl, who runs and hides. Instead of going deep down into the bag, each girl lets the top of her head and her hair show. When the girl who is IT returns, everyone in the bags starts counting all together. The girl who is IT has 15 seconds to guess who is missing.

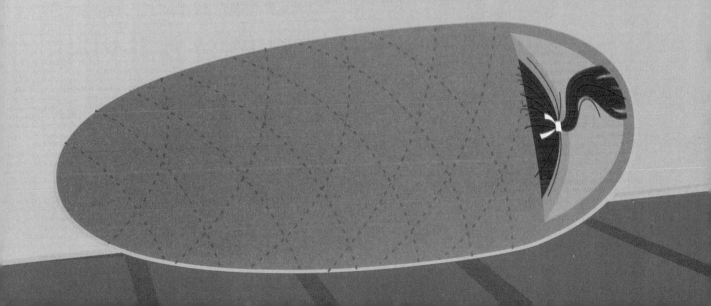

IT'S A GHOST!

This is a game for 2 to 4 players.
The object of this game is to force a player to spell a word.

You need: pencil
              paper (to keep track of the score)

This is how it goes:

1. Player 1 thinks of a word but doesn't say it. For example, if the word she's thinking of is wind, all she says is "w."

2. Player 2 then must think of a word that starts with w and add a letter to it. She thinks of wasp and says, "wa."

3. The third player must think of a word that begins with "wa" but must say the first 3 letters of that word. She might think of waiter and say "wai."

4. THE FOURTH PLAYER IS IN A SPOT NOW. SHE MIGHT SAY "WAIT" AND LOSE THE ROUND BECAUSE SHE SPELLED A COMPLETE WORD. OR SHE COULD THINK OF THE WORD WAIST AND SHE WOULD STILL BE IN THE GAME BY SAYING "WAIS". NOT ONLY WOULD SHE STILL BE IN THE GAME, BUT SHE WOULD HAVE PUT THE NEXT PLAYER IN AN IMPOSSIBLE POSITION. THERE AREN'T TOO MANY WORDS THAT START WITH "WAIS" SO SHE HAS FORCED THE NEXT PLAYER TO SPELL WAIST AND MADE HER LOSE.

5. When a player loses, she gets a G. The next time she loses she will get an H, then an O, then S, T—until she has all the letters to the word GHOST. The last player to become a GHOST is the winner.

ZOO PARADE GAME

Here's one last fun word game.

The first player says the name of an animal. The second player must say an animal whose name begins with the last letter of that first animal's name. For example: The first player says *cow*. The next player says *wallaby*. The third player says *yak*.

Play continues until one player falters and cannot think of an animal that has not already been mentioned. That player drops out of the game. If there are only two players, the one remaining wins.

HEADS UP, SEVENS UP

This game can be played in a classroom if the teacher or monitor says it's okay. Or it can be played at a party.

Seven players stand in the front of the room. The other players lower their heads onto a desk or table and close their eyes. The 7 players quietly sneak around, and each one lightly taps one of the sitting players who has her eyes shut. If a girl is tapped she must put her thumb up.

Then the 7 go back to the front. The 7 say, "Heads up, seven up." Eyes are opened. Each girl that has a thumb up gets to guess which of the 7 touched her. If she guesses right, she goes to the front and the one who touched her sits down. If she guesses wrong, she stays seated and the next girl gets to guess.

Play begins again with a new group of 7 made up of some from the last round who were never guessed and some who are new to the group.